D1708554

Ruth F. Brin

The Story of Esther

illustrated by H. Hechtkopf

Lerner Publications Company
Minneapolis, Minnesota

AN
OUTSTANDING
SELECTION
FROM

Israel

A NOTE ON SOURCES

In preparing this retelling of the Biblical story of Esther, I have consulted the King James Bible, as well as modern Biblical translations, contemporary critics, and the great body of Jewish legend that has grown up around the story of Esther.

Because both modern critics and rabbinical authorities acknowledge that the story of Esther contains some fictional elements, I have used the fairy tale form. I did not have enough space to retell the entire story as it occurs in the Bible. Such details as Mordecai's being a teacher of children, Esther's inviting her friends to the palace, and Jewish women enjoying a higher status than Persian, all come from Talmudic sources.

Historically, Ahasuerus (pronounced uh-*hahz*-you-EE-russ) is probably to be identified as Xerxes I.

Ruth F. Brin

First published in the United States of America 1976
by Lerner Publications Company, Minneapolis, Minnesota

Copyright © 1976 by Massada Press Ltd., Ramat-Gan, Israel

International Standard Book Number: 0–8225–0364–6
Library of Congress Catalog Card Number: 75–743

Printed in Israel and bound in U.S.A.

Long ago, a young Jewish woman named Esther lived in Shushan, the capital of Persia. Esther was an orphan, but her cousin Mordecai took care of her, raising her as his own daughter. In those days, girls dreamed of being beautiful, and Esther *was* beautiful. Girls were not expected to be brave, but we will soon discover that Esther was very brave indeed.

One morning Esther and Mordecai were walking to the school where Mordecai taught Jewish children. On their way, they stopped to watch a most unusual sight. Ahasuerus, the king of Persia, had invited all the princes of the land to come to his palace for a great feast. Now, as Esther and Mordecai watched, they saw the king's guests ride down the main street of Shushan. The richly dressed princes rode in chariots, followed by their wives and daughters, soldiers and servants. It was a magnificent parade.

After the king's guests had passed, Esther and Mordecai hurried on their way to the school. Although the Jews had been conquered long before, Mordecai believed it was his duty to teach the Jewish children of Persia about their religion. Esther helped him by teaching the little ones. Even though it was not the custom, Mordecai had taught Esther everything he had taught the boys. He had done this because he believed that Jewish girls, as well as boys, must learn about their religion.

Mordecai had told Esther that he and she were descendants of the kings of Israel. Sometimes Esther would pretend she was a princess in the court of her ancestor King Saul. But *never* did Esther imagine that she would one day become queen of Persia!

While Esther and Mordecai were busy in their school, the king's party began in the palace. The men gathered in the royal gardens, where the upper branches of the trees interlaced, forming arches. Among the trees, fountains splashed and flowers bloomed. Long tables were set out with colorful linens, golden dishes, and crystal wine goblets. Many kinds of food were served, and there was plenty of wine for all.

Vashti, the queen of Persia, entertained the wives and daughters of the princes inside the palace. She led her guests through all the royal rooms, with their marble floors, silken wall hangings, and tables of gold and silver. The women gasped when they saw Vashti's chests of precious jewels. And when they sat down to eat, each was given a gift of fine perfume.

As night fell on the city, the men in the palace gardens became drunk with wine. When men drink, they often become boastful. And so it was with King Ahasuerus. Speaking of Queen Vashti, the king boasted that she was the "most beautiful woman in the world." Of course, none of the king's guests dared to deny his words. But their silence annoyed Ahasuerus, and he grew angry.

"I will send for Vashti at once!" the king announced. "Then you will see for yourselves how beautiful she is."

The guests listened in silence as the king told his messenger that Vashti was to appear, unveiled, before the company of men. Such a thing was unheard of, for a Persian lady never appeared unveiled before any man except her husband.

Vashti was shocked when she heard the king's command. Rather than obey it, she sent the messenger back to King Ahasuerus, begging him to change his mind. When the king insisted that Vashti appear before him at once, the queen refused. "Never would I do such a thing!" she cried.

Now a wise king can be dangerous to his enemies, but a foolish king can be dangerous to everyone — even to those he loves. Ahasuerus was a very foolish king indeed, and his wife's disobedience made him burn with rage.

"What shall I do?" he asked the princes. "Vashti has defied my orders! She must be punished, but how?"

"Banish her from the kingdom!" yelled one of the princes. "Unless you do this, wives all over the land will defy their husbands when they learn of Vashti's deed."

"You are right," said the foolish king, who by now was quite drunk. "Let Vashti be banished this very night!" After giving the order, the drunken king fell asleep.

When he awoke the next morning, King Ahasuerus was confused about what had happened the night before. Suddenly he remembered the beautiful Vashti, and how he had sent her away forever. Ahasuerus was sorry for what he had done.

Then Haman, a member of the court, came before the king. Haman was both clever and wicked, and he sought to gain more power for himself. "Forget about Vashti," he told the king, "and listen to my plan. Order your messengers to seek out the loveliest young women in the kingdom. Then choose the most beautiful one of all to be your new wife."

The king, who liked games and contests, was pleased with Haman's idea. "Let the search begin at once!" ordered Ahasuerus. "And when it ends, you shall be rewarded, Haman."

When Mordecai heard of the king's search for a new wife, he told Esther that he saw the hand of God in it.

"You will go to the palace," he told Esther, "so that the king might see you and make you his wife. And if it be God's plan, perhaps you will be able to serve our people in some important way."

Esther was amazed. "Me? Become the king's wife? But I'm not beautiful, Mordecai, and I don't want to leave you. Besides, what would a simple girl like me do in the palace?" Esther's heart was filled with fear. But because she loved and trusted Mordecai, Esther did as he had told her. Bidding him goodbye, she entered the gates of the palace.

Esther was led into a huge room where hundreds of beautiful young women from all over the kingdom were assembled. They all waited there until the king sent for them, one by one. Although Esther was too humble to know it, she was the most beautiful of them all. She had large dark eyes, long thick hair, and the graceful walk of a true princess. Many of the girls were the daughters of nobles and princes, and they bragged of their royal descent. But Esther remained silent, never mentioning that she was Jewish, or that King Saul was her ancestor.

At last, it was Esther's turn to go before the king. If Ahasuerus chose her above the others, Esther would become queen of all Persia! Dressed in a simple white gown, she followed the guards through the palace gardens to the throne room. When King Ahasuerus saw her coming, he knew at once that she was the most beautiful woman in his kingdom. Waving the others aside, he declared that Esther would be his queen.

King Ahasuerus and Esther were married the next day. But this is not a story where the king and queen live happily ever after — at least not yet. For King Ahasuerus was still foolish, which made him dangerous. And Haman, who by now was the king's chief adviser, was more wicked and ambitious than ever.

After Esther became queen, she invited seven of the Jewish girls from Mordecai's school to live with her in the palace. Since Esther knew that the king liked games and parties, she and her friends played games with him often. Esther had spent a lot of time playing with the little children at Mordecai's school. So she wasn't surprised that the childish Ahasuerus liked to win every game he played. To make the king happy, Esther saw to it that he always came out the winner.

Mordecai came to the gates of the palace every afternoon after he finished teaching. Esther sent him long notes, and sometimes a package of figs and grapes and freshly baked pastries. Mordecai sent Esther notes, too. He reminded her to observe the Jewish holidays, and he gave her copies of sacred Jewish writings.

Esther enjoyed her life at the palace, for King Ahasuerus was kind to her. But she feared the wicked Haman, who had become almost as powerful as Ahasuerus. In addition to being the king's chief adviser, Haman was now commander of the army and head of the royal treasury. Out of greed, he collected high taxes from the rich and poor alike. And out of pride, he demanded that everyone bow down to him whenever he passed by.

Haman was leading his soldiers through the city one day when he saw Mordecai sitting outside the palace gates. When Haman passed by, Mordecai refused to stand up and bow. Seeing this, Haman strode up to him, his whip in his hand. "The king has ordered every person in this kingdom to bow down to me!" he screamed. "Why do you not obey?"

Mordecai stood up, proud and tall. He was unafraid of Haman, and unimpressed by his shining armor and plumed headdress. "I am a Jew," Mordecai said quietly. "And we Jews bow down only to God, the one true God of heaven and earth."

Haman angrily tapped his boot with his whip. "So," he growled, "you think you can disobey the king's commands! We shall see about this, Jew. *We shall see.*"

Before the day had passed, Haman learned all he could about the Jews. Their religion, he discovered, was nothing like the religion of the Persians. The Jews worshiped their own God, and observed their own holidays and Sabbath. Although they were peaceful people, working on farms and in the cities, Haman began to hate all the Jews because he hated Mordecai. Besides, he believed that if he could destroy the Jews and take their farms and houses, he could become the wealthiest man in Persia.

With this evil plan on his mind, Haman went to see the king. "There is a people in your kingdom who worship their own God," he said, "not yours. They obey their own laws, not yours. These people are called *Jews,* and they must be punished. If we destroy them, taking all their property and possessions, we could greatly increase our wealth."

King Ahasuerus waved a lazy hand. "Do as you like," he said. "Here's my signet ring. Order my lawyers to write a proclamation against the Jews, and seal it with this."

Delighted, Haman went straight to the king's lawyers. With their help, he wrote a proclamation allowing Persians to kill all the Jews in the kingdom — children as well as adults. Their property was to be turned over to Haman and the king. After sealing the proclamation, Haman sent messengers throughout the kingdom to order the destruction of Esther's people.

When Mordecai learned of the terrible order, he hurried to the palace and sent Esther a letter telling her about Haman's proclamation. He told Esther that she must go to the king and beg him to save the Jews.

Esther was afraid. For it was a law that if any person — even the queen — went to see the king without being called, that person would be killed unless the king held out his golden scepter. And recently, the king had held out his scepter only when Haman had told him to.

Before long, Mordecai sent Esther another letter. "Think not that you will be spared in the palace," he wrote. "For if all the Jews are killed, you will be killed, too. Who knows why you became queen, Esther? Perhaps God willed it so that you could save your people from this terrible disaster. Put your life in God's hands, Esther, and do what you must do!"

Now Esther was truly brave. "Ask the Jews to fast and pray for me for three days," she wrote to Mordecai. "My friends and I will do the same. At the end of that time, I will go to the king. And if I perish, I perish."

On the third day, Esther put on the white dress she had worn when the king first saw her. Then, at the risk of her life, Esther approached the throne room. Her friends were weeping because they thought they would never see her again. As Esther walked through the palace, her knees trembling, she began to pray.

King Ahasuerus was sitting on his throne, talking with Haman. Suddenly he looked up and saw Esther, her beautiful dark eyes looking very large because they were brimming with tears.

"Why, Esther," the king said. "What's the matter? If you ask a favor of me, I'll be glad to grant it — anything at all to make you smile." Almost without thinking, the king held out his golden scepter.

Esther was wise as well as brave, and she knew the king well. "I would like to have you — and Haman — come to my apartment tonight for dinner and a party," she said. "Then I'll tell you what is troubling me."

"Of course!" the king replied. "We'll be there at sundown."

Esther thanked the king for his kindness. Then she hurried back through the halls and gardens to talk with her friends about the meal, and about what games she would play with Haman and the king. When everything was prepared, Esther waited for her guests to arrive.

That night they had a wonderful feast, with all the king's favorite foods. Afterward, when the king and Haman were both merry with wine, they played games. As usual, Esther made sure that the king won every game. Then, when Ahasuerus asked her what favor she desired, Esther replied that she wished he and Haman would come again, the next evening.

On the second night, after they had finished with the roast duck, the royal pastries, and the figs and grapes — but *before* they had drunk too much wine — Esther decided it was time to tell the king her problem.

When Ahasuerus again asked her what she wanted, Esther answered: "If you love me, my king, and if you are pleased that I am your wife, then grant me my life and the life of my people."

"What do you mean?" the king demanded. "Who is threatening your life? And who are your people?"

"It has been ordered that we are to be destroyed, my king. Not just enslaved, but killed — every one!"

"And who would order such a thing?" The king was becoming very angry. "Who is he, and where is he?"

Esther pointed at Haman. "This is the enemy," she cried, "the wicked Haman! For I am a *Jew*, and Haman has ordered that all Jews are to be killed."

The king was so angry that he threw his wine goblet on the floor. Then he called his guards and ordered them to take Haman away. "Let Haman be hanged on the gallows he has prepared for the Jews!" the king commanded.

Early the next morning, King Ahasuerus ordered that Esther's cousin Mordecai be brought before him. The king gave his signet ring to Mordecai, making him his chief adviser. The city of Shushan rejoiced, and the Jews had joy and gladness and honor. Mordecai and Esther declared that from then on, the holiday of Purim should be celebrated every spring by all the Jews. And so it is, to this day.

With a wise and kind adviser at his side, even a foolish king like Ahasuerus can become a good ruler and a good husband. So now at last comes the end of Esther's story: *"And they lived happily ever after."*

ESTHER AND THE FEAST OF PURIM

Purim is a feast celebrated by Jews in early spring. It is a delighful holiday on which children dress up in costumes and reenact the story of Esther. It is customary on this day to exchange gifts of cookies and other sweets, and to give money to charity. At the synagogue, the story of Esther is read aloud. When the name of the evil Haman is pronounced, children drown out the sound with rattles and noisemakers. You can see that everyone enjoys this holiday, young and old alike.

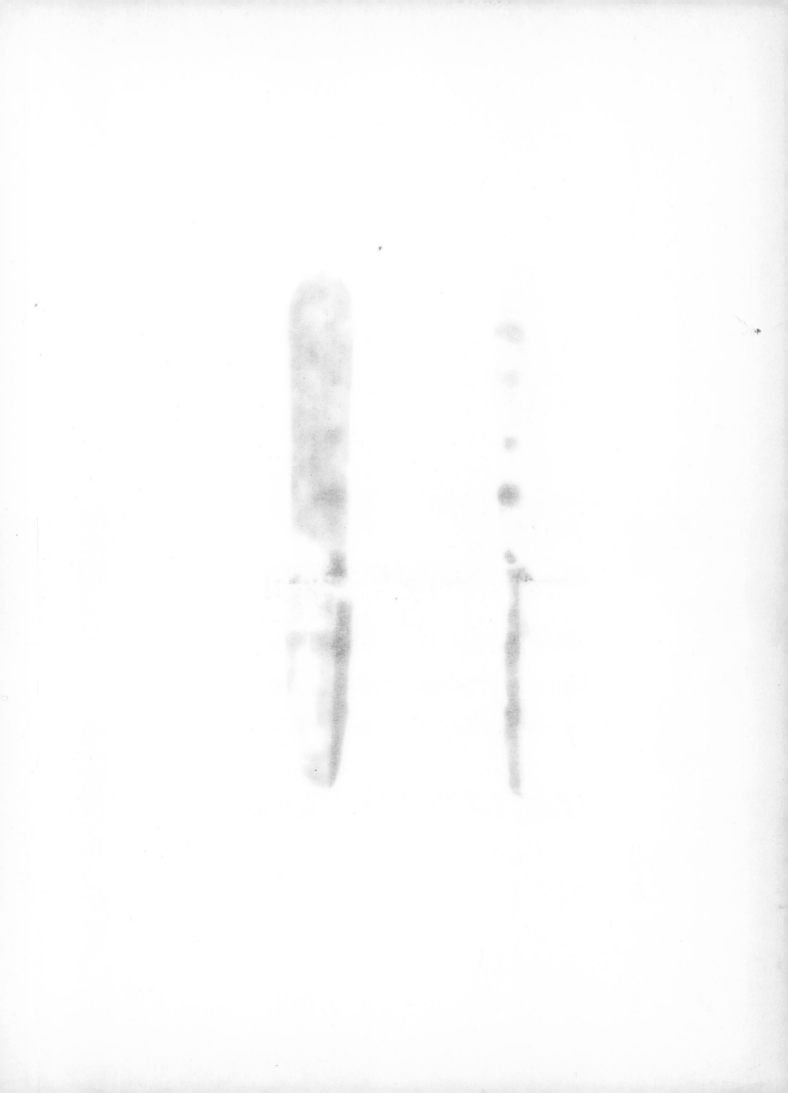

18485

J
244.3
B77s
C.3

18485

Brin, Ruth F.
The story of Esther.

Date Due

MAR 1	MAR 07 '84	FEB 20 '94
NOV 12 78	3/9/84	OCT 3 '94
MAR 18 1979	4/1/84	MAR 13 '95
MAR 9 '8	MAR 06 '85	MAR 13 '9	MAR 18 2011
MAR 7 '8	FEB 24 '86	10 MAR 1008 — March 3
5/16/82	MAR 26 '88	DEC 22 '96
DEC 05 '8		09 MAR 1997
JAN 30 '83	MAR 0	MAR 09 2008
MAR 02 '83	3/17	MAR 15	MAR 15 2015
MAR 20 '83	4/14	MAR 07 '8
FEB 08 '84	MAR. 22 1902	MAR 19 200
FEB 09 2003	MAR 13 2006	FEB 22 2016

MAR 11 2007
MAR 10 2010

Printed in U.S.A.